Parent's Love

and other Islamic Stories

by
Ishrat J Rumy

Illustrated by
Neeta Gangopadhyay

Goodwordkidz

Dedicated to
My beloved daughters
Khadija & Fatima
Who are the source of my inspiration.

Goodword Books Pvt. Ltd.
P. O. Box 3244, Nizamuddin P. O., New Delhi - 110 013
E-mail: info@goodwordbooks.com
Illustrated by Neeta Gangopadhyay
First published 2003   Reprinted 2006
Printed in India
© Goodword Books 2006

Contents

The Prophet's Kindness

Whenever the Prophet Muhammad's followers reaped their first harvest, they brought early, fresh fruits to him. Then he would hand them out to those who sat around him.

One morning, a poor man brought one fruit from his small farm and gave it to the Prophet ﷺ.

The Prophet ﷺ accepted the gift, tasted it and then went on eating it alone while the companions watched.

One of those present meekly said: "O Prophet of Allah, have you overlooked the right of those who watch while you eat?"

The Prophet ﷺ smiled and waited till the man who had brought the fruit had gone.

Then he said: "I tasted the fruit and it was not yet ripe. Suppose I had let you have some of it, someone was bound to say that it tasted bad, and the poor man would have been disappointed. Rather than send him away unhappy. I decided to eat the whole fruit myself."

The Ungrateful Human Being

One day, a man climbed up a tree.

All of a sudden, a strong wind started to blow when he was on one of the top branches.

He was so scared that he felt his heart in his mouth. He raised his head to the sky and prayed: "Oh great God, I promise to sacrifice all my sheep for your cause if I can safely climb down this tree."

"Oh, it seems the wind is not blowing so hard any more ! I think it would be all right, God, if I gave away my sheep's wool for Your cause. Oh, it seems that the wind is becoming weaker and weaker…. God, I shall give away their whey if I reach the ground safe and sound.

"Oh… that wild wind has turned into a breeze now and I've reached the ground quite safely."

"What was I saying….. sheep, wool, whey? What whey? What wool? Who will lose them all? A fool!"

Turning Point

Imam Ghazali was a renowned Muslim scholar who lived in the fifth century of the hijrah. He was born in Tus, a small village near Mashhad.

In those days students who wanted to have a great knowledge of Islam travelled to Nishapur, which boasted several centres of learning and many teachers of repute.

Imam Ghazali, after completing the first part of his education at home, arrived in Nishapur to pursue further studies.

He was brilliant and was soon praised by his tutors as being the most studious and painstaking student. In order not to forget any of the finer points, he formed the habit of noting down all that he heard and learnt from his teachers. And he very carefully rewrote them under various headings and chapters. He treasured these notes as dearly as his life, or perhaps more.

Years later, he decided to return to his village. He tied all his prepared notes into a neat bundle and set forth in the company of a caravan.

On the way, they were held up by a gang of highway thieves who robbed each traveller of all his valuables. And then it was Ghazali's turn. They searched him thoroughly, snatching away all that they wanted, and then laid hands on the tied bundle of notes.

"Take all that you want, but please do not touch this bundle," pleaded Ghazali.

The thieves thought that there must be something very precious hidden in the bundle which Ghazali was trying to save. So they untied it and took it apart. And what did they find? Nothing but a few papers with writing on them.

They asked: "What are these? Of what use are they?"

"Well, they may be of no use to you, but they are of great use to me," Ghazali answered.

"But of what use are they?" the robbers insisted.

"These are the fruits of my labour. If you destroy them, I shall also be destroyed. All my years of work will go down the drain," Ghazali replied.

"So whatever you know is in here, isn't it?" one of them asked.

"Yes."

"Well, knowledge written down on a few pages, which can easily be stolen is no knowledge at all. Go away and think about it and about yourself!"

This casual but stinging remark by a common man shook Ghazali to the core. He realized that he had studied like a parrot, jotting down all that he learned and cramming in into his mind. He found that he knew more, but he thought less. If he wanted to be a true student and a good scholar, he had to absorb knowledge, think, ponder, reason things out and then form his own judgement.

He set out seriously to learn the way he should, and became one of the greatest *ulema* in Islam. But in his old age, when he added up all the worthy things, he said: "The best advice which changed my thinking, was given to me by a highway robber."

An Intelligent Fish Seller

There was a king who was a generous and wonderful man. But his wife was stingy in nature.

Once the king went hunting along with the queen and, on the way, they stopped by a big tree to rest in its shade. There, an Arab brought a fresh big fish to the king. The king was pleased and gave him 4000 dinars for it.

The queen complained immediately: "This is wasting money. It goes far beyond generosity. You spent 4000 dinars for a single fish! How much would you give away if you were given something more precious? If you paid less than that you'd thought inconsiderate and if you wanted to pay more, the treasury would soon be emptied."

She insisted that he had to get the money back from the Arab and pay him the real price of the fish.

"How can I take back what I have already given him? That would not be kingly in manner," exclaimed the king.

"We can trick him and get the money back. For example, we can ask him if the fish is a male or a female. If he says male, we'll immediately say that we were looking for a female, and if he says female, we'll say we were looking for a male. This can be the best excuse to give him back the fish and have the money refunded."

"Oh, very well. You, Arab man, come over here and tell me if it was a male or a female fish."

The clever Arab, who promptly understood the reasoning behind the question, replied: "It was neuter, Sir."

The king liked his response and ordered that he be given another 4000 dinars.

The man was quite happy to receive another 4000 dinars. When he turned around to leave he dropped a coin. He bent down and picked it up.

The queen took advantage of this to say to the king:"Look, how mean he is. He didn't leave a single coin for anybody else."

The king said, "Hey you, come over here again. I gave you thousands of dinars but even so, when one of your coins dropped, you bent down and picked that single coin up. Don't you feel ashamed of yourself?"

The man gently replied, "Long live our king. I didn't do it because I'm a stingy person. It's just that the coin bears a picture of your Majesty on it, and I thought it would be an insult to leave it on the ground to be stepped on by careless people."

The king was so very grateful that he granted him another 4000 dinars.

The Tongue

Luqman, who was a wise person, served an officer when he was a young boy.

One day, his master said: "Slaughter one of the sheep and roast the best part of its meat for me."

Luqman obeyed his order and roasted the tongue of the sheep for his master.

The next day, the master called Luqman and said: "Roast the worst part of a sheep today."

Luqman again roasted the tongue of a sheep for his master.

When the officer sat down to eat, he was startled to see the roasted tongue again. He felt curious and wanted to know the reason.

Luqman said: "If a tongue is truthful and honest, then it is the best part of the body. But when a tongue tells lies and utters dishonest words, then it is the worst part of the body."

The Bad Omen

Once a king who had only one eye went out hunting.

When he was almost at the city gate, he saw a one-eyed man who was about to come in.

All of a sudden the king felt bad and considered the coincidence an evil omen.

He called out to his soldiers and commanded: "Lay hold of that one-eyed man and tie him to one of these columns. I shall tell you what to do on my return."

That day the king was successful in hunting, for he was able to kill lots of birds and animals.

When the king came back to the city gate, the poor one-eyed man saw him and the heap of game on the carriage behind him.

So he shouted : "Which of us was an evil omen for the other? I or you? I saw you and so I was tied and left under the hot sun, while you saw me and God Almighty bestowed upon you so many blessings!".

The king smiled, set him free and granted him a good remand.

A Fleeting Moment

Mutawakkil, the cruel Abbasid Khalifah, was very fearful because people were so drawn to Imam Hadi. He was very upset by the fact that people were ready to do anything that the Imam ordered.

Conspirators also gathered around the Khalifah and told him that perhaps the Imam intented to revolt, and that they might find some evidence in his house.

So Mutawakkil ordered some of his cruel henchmen to break into the Imam's house, and search it then arrest him without any warning in the middle of the night when all were asleep. Mutawakkil made this decision while he was at a banquet and was drinking heavily.

Mutawakkil's men entered the Imam's house. They found him alone in a room sitting on a carpet on the gravel of the floor, deep in remembrance of Allah. They searched everywhere, but couldn't find anything. So they arrested the Imam and took him to Mutawakkil.

When the Imam arrived, Mutawakkil was at the peak of his drinking bout. He ordered the Imam to sit by him. Then he offered him a glass of wine.

The Imam refused and said : "By Allah, never has wine entered my body. Excuse me from drinking it."

Mutawakkil agreed, but said: "Then sing for us and entertain us with beautiful poems."

The Imam said: "I am not interested in poetry and I remember only little of the poems of others."

Mutawakkil said: "That is no excuse, you must recite some poetry."

So the Imam began:

They made rising mountains their residence
And they always had armed men guarding them.
But none could save them from the attack of death.
At the end they were brought down, humbled, from those hills
And placed in the misery of deeply dug graves,
At this time a caller called: Where is all that glory, crowns and luxury?
Where is the face that knew comfort and hid itself behind silk curtains
From the gaze of the commoner? The grave disgraced them at end.
Those delicate faces are the ground for worms to crawl on.
For a long time they sucked, swallowed, drank and ate of the earth.
But today they are food for the earth and its pests.

The Imam's words rang out and so affected his audience with their depth that the wine completely lost its effect on them.

Mutawakkil threw his glass away and started crying.

Thus the Khalifah's banquet was ruined and the light of truth shone into diseased hearts, even if it were only for a fleeting moment.

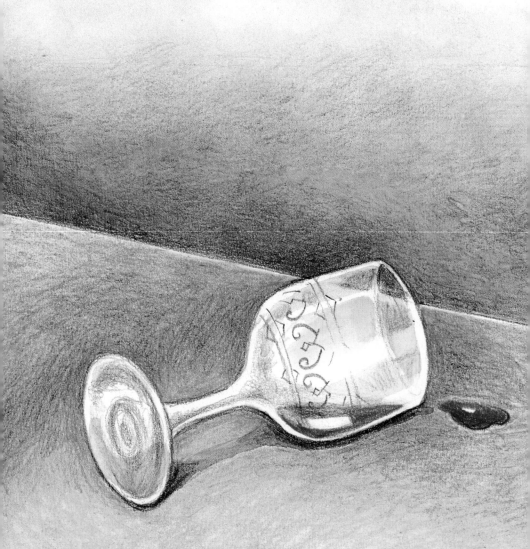

Tit for Tat

A thief who believed in heavenly determinism once broke into a garden and climbed a tree to pick some fruits.

While he was eating the fruit on the branch of the tree, the owner of the garden suddenly appeared and shouted angrily: "Who are you? What are you doing there?"

"A subject of God is on a tree of God and with a hand of God is picking and eating the fruit of God," answered the thief.

The gardener made him climb down the tree and tied him to a tree trunk. He then started to beat him with a thick stick. The thief, now in terrible pain, cried out: "Why are you beating me?"

"The stick of God in the hand of God is striking a subject of God," the gardener answered.

A Meaningful Discussion

The common people considered Behlool a madman, though he was not mad. Junaid, a scholar of repute, knew him very well.

One day when they met, Junaid requested Behlool to give him some guidance.

"You don't need any advice. You are a well known scholar," said Behlool.

But Junaid insisted. Behlool gave in and said: "Well, I'll ask you three questions. Give the correct answers and that will be your advice."

And then he proceeded to ask:

> "Do you know how to talk?
> Do you know how to eat?
> Do you know how to sleep?"

Junaid found these questions. He said: "I know how to talk. I talk with a low voice, politely and to the point, so that the listeners are not at all offended.

I eat after washing my hands, say *Bismillah* before I commence, and chew the food properly. When I finish, I thank Allah.

Before I go to sleep, I do my *wudhu* and retire to a clean bed. Then I bear witness to my faith and sleep."

Behlool stood up and started walking away, saying: "I thought you were quite learned. You don't know even the most elementary things about Islam."

But Junaid would not let him go. "Please guide me," he said.

"Well," said Behlool, "It's no use talking softly if you are telling a lie.

Remembering Allah before eating has no meaning if the food you eat is forbidden, or the food has been bought by unlawful income or with the money of an orphan, a widow or a fellow man. And what is the use of sleeping after doing *wudhu* and saying prayer, if your heart is full of malice, jealousy and enmity towards your brother in faith?"

28

Sound Judgement

As usual, the Prophet Dawud ﷺ also known as David, was solving the problems of his people when two men, one of whom had a field came to him.

The owner of the field said: "O dear Prophet, this man's sheep came to my field at night and ate up the grapes and I have come to ask for compensation."

Dawud ﷺ asked the owner of the sheep: "Is this true?"

"Yes, sir," he answered.

Dawud ﷺ said: "I have decided that you will give him your sheep in exchange for the field."

At that time, the eleven-year-old son of the Prophet, Sulaiman ﷺ, known as Solomon, spoke up: "I have another opinion. The owner of the sheep should take the field to cultivate until the grapes grow again, while the other man takes the sheep and makes use of their wool and milk until his field is restored. If the grapes grow and the field returns to its former state, then the field owner should take back his field and give the sheep back to their owner."

The Prophet Dawud ﷺ answered: "This is a sound judgement. Praise be to Allah for gifting you with wisdom. You are truly Sulaiman the wise."

Nobody Cares for Me !

A man was on his death bed. The family understood that he was passing away. So the family members and relatives began to weep sitting around him.

Suddenly the sick man spoke out: "All of you be quiet! Oh, dear father! Why are you crying?"

"My son! I'm crying because I'll break down and be lonely if you leave," replied the grief-stricken father.

"Mother dear! Why are you crying?" asked the ill man.

"Oh, my dear son, I always hoped that you would assist me in my old age, but you are leaving before me," replied the mother.

"What makes you cry, my dear wife?"

"My children are going to be orphaned. I shall have to look after them all alone, without your warm companionship. I can't stop the tears."

"And why are you weeping, my dear children?"

"Who will take care of us and provide our livelihood after you are gone?" answered one of the children.

"Alas! What a pity! I have given my whole life to you all. Today my soul is leaving my body, I am going to leave you forever, but all one of you are crying for your own sakes and worried about your own future. Nobody is worried about me or about what awaits me." At this moment the man closed his eyes and died.

Malik–e–Ashter

A tall and well built man with a tanned face and a healed cut on his eyebrow that told a tale of warfare, strode purposefully through the market place.

A merchant threw a handful of waste at him just to provide a moment's entertainment in the market. But the man continued to walk on as before without batting an eyelid.

Another merchant went up to the offender and asked: "Do you know the man whom you just offended?"

"No. I don't know him. He was one of the thousands who pass by us every day. Who was he, anyway?"

"Seriously, didn't you recognize him? This passer by happened to be the general commander Malik-e-Ashtar."

"Was that man Malik-e-Ashtar? Was that the man whose name startles people and shakes his enemies?"

"Yes, that was Malik."

"Alas! What did I just do? He might just give orders now for me to be severely punished. I'll run after him and beg him to forgive me.'

He ran after Malik, and noting that he went towards a Masjid, he followed him there. There, he saw him stand to say prayer. He waited till Malik was done.

Then the merchant went to him and introduced himself all the while crying and apologizing to Malik. He said: "I am the one who offended you."

Malik said: "By Allah, I came to the Masjid for you. I understand that you are misguided and unwise, that you bother people without a reason. I felt sad for you. I came to the Masjid to pray for your guidance to the right path. I had no intention of harming you, as you probably thought."

Clever Talk

Once a proud man dismounted from his horse in front of his friend's house to pay him a visit.

He saw a boy standing close to his horse and so he said to him:

"Hey you, lad, come on over here."

"Me?…. Yes, Sir."

"Come and take hold of the bridle of this horse. Hold on to it until I return from my friend's house."

"But excuse me, Sir, does this horse bite?"

"No, it doesn't."

"How about kicking? Does it kick?"

"Of course not."

"I'm sorry, but may I ask you if it runs away."

"No, my boy, it doesn't run away either."

"Such a good horse that doesn't bite, kick or run away, won't need someone to guard it. Leave it here and let it move around freely and be sure it won't go anywhere."

The boy then turned around and calmly walked away.

The Devil's Attempt

A man once dreamt of Satan.

Satan was holding some frayed ropes and broken chains and he was fuming with anger.

In his dream, the man felt curious and asked the devil: "Hey, devil, why are you carrying these things?"

The devil answered: "I trap people and drag them along with these ropes and chains."

"Why are you looking so furious?" the man wanted to know.

"Tonight, I intended to drag Sheikh Ansari towards me and to evil but, I failed. Each time I pulled on the ropes or chains, they snapped. I did this seven times, but the result was just the same. Now I am very disappointed about the Sheikh."

In the morning, the man rushed to the Sheikh without delay and informed him about the dream.

"Alhamdulillah, God has saved me," said the Sheikh, "Last night, my wife's labour pains started. I needed some money to buy the required medicines and things. But I had no money at home, except some money which I was holding in trust for someone. I told myself that the owner of the money would be pleased to lend some of it to me at such a time.

But I was prudent and decided not to take any of it. I hesitated seven times and, finally, I became firmly determined not to take the money. Almighty God then eased the delivery pains and my wife had no serious problem in giving birth to our child."

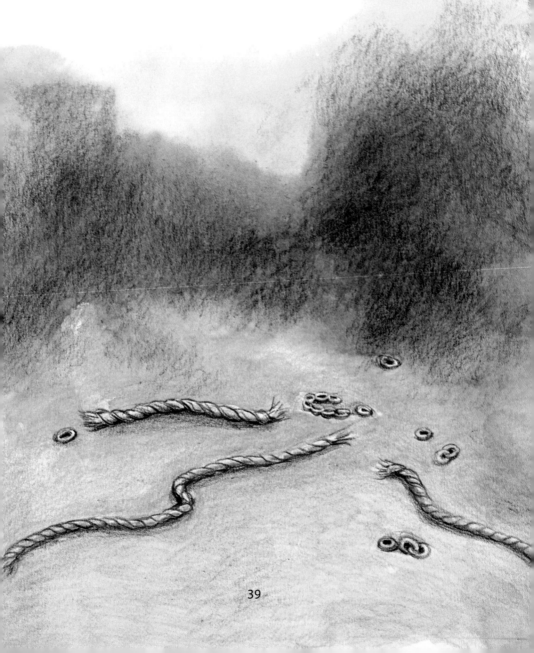

Follow Your Heart

One beautiful spring morning, a farmer and his son were taking their donkey to the market to sell it.

The father and his son were walking along together and the donkey was following them. They had not walked far when they passed a group of girls coming from the opposite direction.

"Just look at that," laughed one of the girls, pointing to the farmer. "What foolish people! They walk along the road when they could ride on their donkey!"

The old man quietly told his son to get on the donkey's back and they continued walking towards the market. Next they passed a group of men sitting by the side of the road, talking among themselves.

"See what I mean?" said one of the men, as the farmer and his son passed by. "The young have no respect for their old parents any more. Get down you lazy boy, and let your father rest his legs !"

The son jumped down from the donkey's back and his father rode on the donkey. Soon they came across some women and children.

"Look at that cruel man!" they exclaimed. "He is riding so fast that the poor boy can hardly keep up with him."

41

The farmer stopped and lifted the boy up behind him. They continued on their way and had almost reached the market when they met a shopkeeper on the road.

"Is that your own donkey?" asked the shopkeeper.

"Yes," replied the farmer.

"Then I'm surprised at how you are treating him," said the shopkeeper.

"Two people on the back of one donkey is too many. He is sure to die from the strain. You should carry him instead!"

By this time, the farmer was getting used to taking other people's advice. He and his son got off the donkey and tied its legs together. Then they tied the rope to a long pole and carried the donkey upside down. But their donkey didn't want to be carried. By kicking and struggling, the donkey broke the rope holding his feet. He fell into a river near the road and was drowned. There was nothing the farmer could do except return home.

"Next time," said the farmer angrily," I'll please myself."

43

Insha Allah

A man was heading for the market with enough money to buy a donkey. On the way, he saw one of his friends.

"Where are you going?" asked the friend.

"I'm going to the market to buy a donkey."

"Say 'Insha Allah' (God willing) before you hope to do anything," advised the friend.

"Come on, no need to say that. My money is right here with me and there are a lot of donkeys in that market," replied the man.

His friend only shrugged and didn't say anything more. The man began walking towards the market. On the way, a thief stole his money bag and he didn't find out until he had reached the market.

All of a sudden, he realized that his money was gone, and he had no choice but to go back home.

On the way he saw his friend again.

"Where are you coming from? What happened?" asked the friend.

"I'm coming from the market, Insha Allah! I was robbed of my money, Insha Allah!"

Three Arm Lengths for Everyone

Behlool liked to visit the graveyards. "People here are good friends," he used to say. "They do not backbite."

Once, he sat in a corner of a graveyard. With a long stick he started prodding at some of the old skulls which were scattered around.

Harun Rashid, the king, passed by and saw him.

"O Behlool! What are you doing?"

"Oh, nothing very important," said Behlool, "I am just trying to find out whether the skulls belong to kings or paupers. They are all the same."

"And what is the stick for?" Harun asked.

"Well, I am measuring the earth," replied Behlool.

"Measuring the earth? What are your findings?" Harun joked.

"It is one and the same, O king," Behlool retorted. "Three arm lengths for me, in spite of my poverty, and three arm lengths for you, in spite of your pomp and wealth."

A Parent's love

Once, for some reason, a king gave orders for a father and his son to be thrashed.

"Tie them to those columns and give them each a hundred strokes with that cane. Start with the father, that would be much better."

The guard said to the father: "Stand still old man. Let me tie you. Now be ready for I'm starting, 1, 2, 3, ………………..98, 99, 100."

"All right, that's enough. Now it's the son's turn, tie him up and beat him," said the king.

"Come on boy, stand beside this column and give me your hands," said the guard.

"Oh, no, please, for God's sake, don't beat my son. Stop beating," the father pleaded.

"Huh! You endured a hundred strokes without saying so much as a word. But now that your son is being beaten, how is it that you're wailing and weeping?" exclaimed the king.

"The first hundred strokes were not too hard to bear, but these strokes are tearing my heart apart. I can't stand the pain."

Khalifah Ali

One day Khalifah Ali was carefully recording all the money that came into the treasury and all that was spent from it by the light of a candle.

At that time, Talha and Jubair came to him for personal reasons.

When they sat down, Ali lit another candle and put out the first candle.

The guests exchanged a glance of surprise and then one of them asked: "O Ali, we have come on some important business. But why did you put out the first candle?"

"That was a candle bought with Treasury funds. As long as I worked for the treasury, I used it. Now you have come for some personal work, so I use the candle bought from my personal fund," replied the Khalifah.

Rooting Out a Problem

Once upon a time an emperor bought some very old china ware which he liked very much.

One day a slave of his dropped one of the china dishes which of course broke into pieces.

The emperor became very angry and shouted: "Hey, executioner. Come quickly and kill this slave, for he has broken my precious dish!"

There was a man in the palace who, noticing what happened, turned to the emperor and said: "Your Majesty, please forgive him.

I have a special kind of substance which, if applied to broken china, can restore it to its former state."

"Really?"

"Yes. But I must first see the rest of your precious china ware. Then I shall start sticking together the broken pieces of china for you."

"All right, here are the rest of my precious china dishes."

"Fine! Now I'm going to mend it."

But instead of mending the china bowl, he started breaking other dishes as well.

"What are you doing? You have broken all the china ware! I must give orders for you to be killed too, but first tell me why you have done this?"

"As I was sure that these dishes would cause the death of many other innocent people, I decided to break all the china ware so that you would only kill me. This way one would be killed instead of many."

The emperor thought for a while and realized that he was right. So he forgave the slave too and set them free.

55

The Guide of Life

Before Abu 'Ali ibn-e Sina was even twenty years of age, he had already learned everything there was to know in those days. He was the most learned person of his times in religion, natural sciences and mathematics.

One day, he went to Abu 'Ali ibn Maskooya, a very famous scholar. Arrogantly, he threw a walnut to him and asked him to work out its area.

Ibn Maskooya gave him a few booklets by Taharat al A'raq on the importance of correct behaviour. He said: "Mend your ways and then I will work out the area of the walnut. You are more in need of improvement than I am of determining the area of this walnut."

Ibn Sina felt ashamed of himself and allowed this rebuke to guide him throughout his life.

A Wise Shepherd

A shepherd was busy grazing his sheep in a meadow. A learned man who was passing by realized that the shepherd was illiterate.

So he said to him: "Why don't you seek knowledge so that you may become a literate and learned man?"

The shepherd replied: "I've learnt the best parts of all sciences, so I don't need to go any further on this course."

"Tell me what is it you've learnt?"

"There are four things we should know:

First, not to lie so that truthfulness may reign.

Second, not to find fault with anyone, as long as I'm full of faults myself.

Third, not to eat prohibited food as long as there is permitted food for me.

And finally, never to neglect the devil's deceit and trickery, until I step into the land of paradise."

The One Closer to God

Once upon a time, there was a holy man who lived all alone in the mountains and worshipped God al the time.

He believed that in this way he could be much closer to God.

Once he was told in his dreams to go to the town and visit a shoemaker who was working there whom God loved.

The holy man did so, and when he met the shoemaker, he said: "Hail to you old man." Then he asked: "What do you do?"

The shoemaker said: "As you see, I'm a shoemaker. I pray to God, keep the fast and repair or make shoes. I give part of my income to the poor as alms and the rest to my family and household to live on."

"Of course these are all good things to do, but going away and giving oneself up to God away from everything and everyone is quite different and definitely has a higher value," thought the holy man.

He then returned to his place in the mountains and went on with his worshipping tasks.

At night, he was told in a dream to go to the shoemaker once more and ask him why his face was so lit up.

The next morning, he met the shoemaker and asked: "What makes your face shine as it does, old man?"

"Nothing. I only consider whoever I meet as the people who will finally be saved and myself as the one who will not."

A Satanic Calculation

Imam Jafar Sadik became interested in a man after he had repeatedly heard about his piety and kindness and his popularity with the common people.

The Imam decided to find out if the man was truly righteous.

So, one day, the Imam went to observe him. At that time, the man was surrounded by people. After a while, the people left and the man began to walk away. The Imam followed him.

A little later, the man entered a bakery and cleverly hid two loaves of bread under his robe while the baker was busy. The Imam was surprised to see this and thought that the man must have paid for the loaves earlier.

Even so, the Imam felt disturbed by the way the man had taken the bread without letting the baker know.

The man came out of the bakery and walked ahead. The Imam followed him. Soon, the man stopped by a fruit stand. As soon as the fruit vendor looked the other way, the man took two pomegranates, hurriedly hid them under his robe then left.

The astonished Imam continued to follow him and was surprised to see that the man gave the bread and fruit to a sick man.

The Imam couldn't wait any more. He went to the man and told him everything he had seen and asked him to explain his strange behaviour. The man said: "I assume that you're Jafar ibn-e Muhammad."

"Yes, I'm Jafar ibn-e Muhammad."

"I'm sorry to say that you're very ignorant."

"How can you say that?"

"Your question shows your sheer ignorance. Obviously, you can't do a simple sum. Don't you know that Allah says in the Quran: Whoever does a good deed shall be rewarded ten times over. The Quran also says that whoever commits an evil deed, he will be punished only once for it. I stole two loaves of bread, which meant two sins. Then I stole two pomegranates that meant two more sins, altogether four sins. But I gave the two loaves and the two pomegranates for the cause of Allah. Each counts as ten good deeds. Thus I have forty good deeds to my credit, and forty minus four is thirty-six. Like this, I have thirty-six pure good deeds to my name. This is simple arithmetic but you cannot understand it."

The Imam answered: "Your calculation shows how very ignorant you are. You should know that Allah only accepts the deeds of the pious. Now a simple piece of arithmetic should be enough to make you aware of your mistake. As you say, you committed four sins. Also since you've given stolen goods to people in the name of charity and good will, you have not earned any good points but, instead

have a sin against your name for each deed. So, you have a total of eight sins. Moreover, you have done no good deeds."

The man was left speechless, as the Imam walked away, he gazed after him in a state of shock.

Burden and Patience

Once upon a time there were two friends, one of whom was tolerant by nature while the other was impatient.

One day, when they were carrying baskets full of fruits on their heads from their village to a nearby town to sell, the impatient one soon started to complain: "Hey, I'm tired. I can't go on, I can't stand this any more."

"Are you serious? We've just started!" exclaimed the tolerant man.

"Anyway, I can't go on."

"I wonder why you're like this!"

"I know your load is heavier than mine and you're not stronger than me either. But I don't understand how you can laugh and be happy while you're carrying it!"

"You know, I've put a kind of plant on my load which lightens it and makes it quite easy for me to bear."

"Really! Is that right? Can you give me a piece of that plant?"

"Certainly. It is the plant of patience which lightens any load."

Faulty Punishment

Once a man committed a crime during the reign of Mamoon.

The king gave orders for the wrongdoer to be arrested, but he ran away. So his brother was arrested instead and brought to the king.

"Now tell us where your brother is, or we'll hang you instead of him," said Mamoon.

"Suppose one of your soldiers was about to behead me and you ordered him to set me free, would he do so?" asked the brother.

"Of course he would."

"Then I too have brought you an order from a great king whom you shall obey and follow."

"Who is that king and what is his order?"

"He is the one and only God, of course, who has said that no one should be punished for the sin of another."

Mamoon ordered him to be set free.

Death

The Prophet Sulaiman ﷺ was a king. He was given an extraordinary kingdom by Allah, and he ruled over the winds and the waves. All men, jinn and animals had to obey him.

One day, the Prophet Sulaiman ﷺ decided to survey his people. He ordered his subjects to arrange themselves in a manner that would enable him to view them. He went to his palace and there on a roof he stood alone to inspect them. No one was permitted to come near. Just then, a man appeared.

"Who are you? Don't you know that no one is supposed to enter here?" asked the Prophet.

"I need no permission for entry. It is your Lord's command that your time on earth is over," answered the angel.

And so Sulaiman ﷺ died. But his subjects did not know. They thought that the king was still judging them. Then Allah sent some worms which ate through the staff on which Sulaiman ﷺ was leaning. The staff broke and Sulaiman's ﷺ fell to the ground.

Only then did his people became aware of his death.

The Advice of the Prophet Idris

The Prophet Idris ﷺ, also known as Enoch in the Bible, was of the fifth generation of the Prophet Adam ﷺ. It is reported that he was the first to invent the basic form of writing. Some of his wise sayings are:

"Happy is he who looks at his own deeds and appoints them as pleaders to his lord."

"None can show better gratitude for Allah's favours than he who shares them with others."

"Do not envy people for what they have, as they will enjoy it only for a short while."

"He who indulges in excess will not benefit from it."

"The real joy of life is to have wisdom."

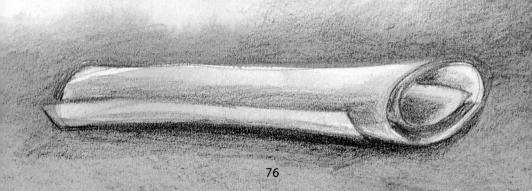

Other Children's Books

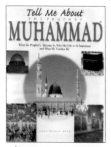 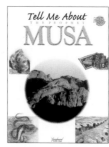  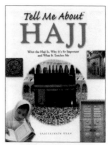

LIFE BEGINS
Quran Stories for Little Hearts

THE FIRST MAN
Quran Stories for Little Hearts

THE TWO BROTHERS
Quran Stories for Little Hearts

ALLAH'S BEST FRIEND
Quran Stories for Little Hearts

THE TRAVELS OF THE PROPHET IBRAHIM
Quran Stories for Little Hearts

THE ARK OF NUH
Quran Stories for Little Hearts

THE BRAVE BOY
Quran Stories for Little Hearts

THE ANT'S PANIC
Quran Stories for Little Hearts

THE QUEEN AND THE BIRD
Quran Stories for Little Hearts

A UNIQUE MIRACLE
Quran Stories for Little Hearts

THE SLEEPERS IN THE CAVE
Quran Stories for Little Hearts

THE IRON WALL
Quran Stories for Little Hearts

THE MOST PATIENT MAN
Quran Stories for Little Hearts

THE PIOUS MAN
Quran Stories for Little Hearts

THE TWO GARDENS
Quran Stories for Little Hearts

The Kingdom of Allah
Allah Gives Us Food

Quran Stories for Young Readers
The Kindness of the Queen

Quran Stories for Young Readers
Prophet Muhammad ﷺ Receives the First Revelation

Quran Stories for Young Readers
The Camel and the Evil People

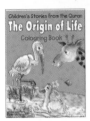
Children's Stories from the Quran
The Origin of Life
Colouring Book

Children's Stories from the Quran
Ark of Nuh and the Animals
COLOURING BOOK

Children's Stories from the Quran
First Man on the Earth
COLOURING BOOK

Children's Stories from the Quran
The Two Sons of Adam
COLOURING BOOK

Children's Stories from the Quran
The Brave Boy
COLOURING BOOK

Children's Stories from the Quran
Tale of A Fish
COLORING BOOK

Children's Stories from the Quran
The Ant's Panic
COLORING BOOK

Children's Stories from the Quran
The Queen and the Bird
COLORING BOOK

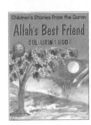
Children's Stories from the Quran
Allah's Best Friend
COLOURING BOOK

Children's Stories from the Quran
The Story of the Prophet Ibrahim
COLOURING BOOK

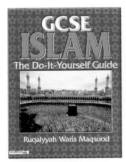
GCSE ISLAM
The Do-It-Yourself Guide
Ruqaiyyah Waris Maqsood

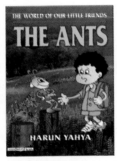
THE WORLD OF OUR LITTLE FRIENDS
THE ANTS
HARUN YAHYA

HONEYBEES
THAT BUILD PERFECT COMBS
HARUN YAHYA

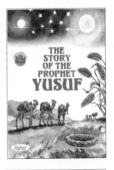
THE STORY OF THE PROPHET YUSUF

Goodword
Islamic Studies
1
A Graded Course

Goodword
Islamic Studies
2
A Graded Course

Goodword
Islamic Studies
6
A Graded Course

Children's Stories from the Quran
The Ark of Nuh and the Great Flood
Sticker Book

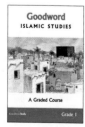
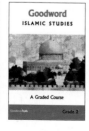
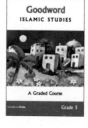

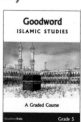